APOSTOLIC
CATALYST

**UNDERSTANDING
KINGDOM
FUNDAMENTALS**

DR. FREDERICK D. ACKLIN

Copyright © 2021 by Dr. Frederick D. Acklin. All rights reserved. No part of this publication may be reproduced, distributed, or transmitted in any form or by any means, including photocopying, recording, or other electronic or mechanical methods, without the prior written permission of the publisher, except in the case of brief quotations embodied in critical reviews and certain other noncommercial uses permitted by copyright law. For permission requests, write to the publisher, addressed "Attention: Permissions Coordinator," at the address below.

ISBN: 978-1-7372246-2-4

Publishing By: DemiCo National, LLC

www.DemiCoNational.com

TABLE OF CONTENTS

Forward By Apostle Stephen A. Davis *(Page 7)*

1. Catch The Revelation (Page 9)
2. Acquisition of Kingdom *(Page 19)*
3. The Fundamentals of Kingdom *(Page 28)*
4. Actualization of Vision *(Page 39)*
5. Leadership Branches *(Page 46)*
6. Yokes and Yielding Submission *(Page 42)*
7. Systems and Strategy *(Page 58)*
8. Teams and Generations *(Page 65)*

Forward

First of all, I would like to commend Apostle Fredrick Acklin on this work that will align hearts and minds for untold wisdom and possessions. By expanding the kingdom of God from an inherited place reserved for those who have passed on; Apostle Acklin establishes the concept that God's kingdom is for here and now for those who dare to embrace it.

While reading this book, you will experience a paradigm shift intellectually and spiritually. This shift is common for individuals who obtain a kingdom revelation.

Simon Peter encountered this revelation and became the foundation of the New Testament Church. This book will position you to become the foundation of something that will transform the world we live in. Within every individual, there is undiscovered greatness waiting for the right tools for that greatness to be released. You are now reading a valued tool that is sure to reveal your inner potential that will change your generation.

Christ Forever,

Apostle Stephen A. Davis

CHAPTER ONE

CATCH THE REVELATION

The Revelation

In order to enter into the kingdom, we must be born again, followed by that we need a personal revelation to extract the wisdom of God. Peter had a revelation straight from God about Christ and His real identity. This information was hidden in plain sight, for they all saw the miracles, but only one caught the revelation. Revelation flows and hoovers over the earth awaiting someplace to reside. Jesus said it like this, "The son of man has no place to lay His head" What was he speaking of?

I heard a great man of God explain this truth to be that "Jesus had no place to allow his concepts, thoughts, ideas and kingdom principles where they would be received and appreciated." Apostle Reginald Lewis

- Mark 4: 10-12, As soon as Jesus was alone with the Twelve and those around Him, they asked Him about the parable. And He told them, "The mystery of the kingdom of God has been given to you, but to those on the outside, everything is expressed in parables, so that, 'they may be ever seeing but never perceiving, and ever hearing but never understanding; otherwise, they might turn and be forgiven.

Misconceptions of the Kingdom

The early church viewed believers as initiators, Spirit-led, active ministers. Today we too often view believers as followers, man-led, passive attendees.

The early church viewed leaders as fathers, servants, resources, and equippers who said, "Go, we will train you." Today we too often view leaders as directors, visionaries, gatherers, and ministers who say, "Come, we'll minister to you."

For the kingdom of God is not in word, but in power. Many think that attending church, praising God, giving tithes, and acting righteously is the kingdom. Let me say assuredly that's really not it. The bible defines the kingdom as this:

- Romans 14:7 - For the kingdom of God is not meat and drink; but righteousness, and peace, and joy in the Holy Ghost. Rom 14:7

- Daniel 2:44- And in the days of these kings shall the God of heaven set up a kingdom, which shall never be destroyed: and the kingdom shall not be left to other people, but it shall break in pieces and consume all these kingdoms, and it shall stand forever.

Scriptural Kingdom Requirements

- John 3:3 – Verily, verily I say unto you, except a man be born again he cannot see the Kingdom of God.

- Matthew 18:3 – Except ye become as little children, ye shall in no wise enter the Kingdom of Heaven.

- Luke 4:43 – And he [Jesus] said unto them, I must preach the kingdom of God to other cities also: for therefore am I sent.

- Luke 8:10 – And he [Jesus] said, unto you it is given to know the mysteries of the kingdom of God:

Kingdom Members-

The word Ekklesia referred to people selected, called out from the general populace, to serve in a civil capacity as a governing arm or cabinet of a governor or king: technically, "a civil body of selected officials."

Yes, we're called out of darkness into light but more specifically (and accurately) we're selected to serve as the "cabinet of the King," Jesus' governing arm on the earth: the governmental executive of the Kingdom. If this doesn't stir your imagination and inflame the fire in your heart, then nothing will!

Kingdom Reign

Jesus envisioned a prevailing Ekklesia – a cabinet of the King – against whom even the "gates of Hades" – a reference to the counsel or cabinet of systemic evil – would not prevail. The prophet Isaiah had foreseen this holy moment declaring that "the government" rests on Jesus' shoulder and that "of the increase of His government and peace there will be no end" Isaiah 9:6, 7

The Ekklesia, by definition, then has nothing to do with some denominational affiliation or a brick-and-mortar building and is not the meeting that takes place on some day of the week.

The Ekklesia has everything to do with being a Kingdom community; a redeemed family, centered on the King, advancing the Kingdom of God in their collective sphere of influence, knowing their Christ-centered personal lives woven together into a Christ-filled communal life ought to be the "pillar and foundation of the truth" (1 Timothy 3:15 c. Colossians 2:2, 3).

For sure, such a community will meet – often and in various ways – but their meetings don't define or restrict them; their meetings are an overflow of who they are: alive in the Spirit, in love with one another and on mission together.

God's Ekklesia is a Kingdom priesthood of all believers. Peter captured this theme so well too. He taught, using Old Testament language, that we "as living stones, are being built up a spiritual house, a holy priesthood, to offer up spiritual sacrifices acceptable to God through Jesus Christ" (1 Peter 2:5). He then, marvelously, declared: "But you are a chosen generation, a royal priesthood, a holy nation, His own special people, that you may proclaim the praises of Him who called you out of darkness into His marvelous light" (1 Peter 2:9). The language is unmistakable. God's desire expressed in Exodus 19:5, 6 is fulfilled in us!

The purpose of a priest is to minister to God and, of course, any true ministry to God overflows in ministry to others. The Old Testament priesthood was certainly involved in all kinds of ministry to people, but the point is obvious: the priesthood exists first and foremost to minister to God, not to serve as mediators between God and others. While God tolerated the second-hand, mediated relationship in the Old Covenant; He does not in the New Covenant, a covenant sealed by the blood of His Son: the one and only Mediator. "For there is one God and one Mediator between God and men, the Man Christ Jesus" (1 Timothy 2:5).

Scripture References

- 1 Corinthians 1:24- But to them which are called, both Jews and Greeks, Christ the power.

- 1 Corinthians 2:4- And my speech and my preaching was not with enticing words of man's.
- Romans 1:16- For I am not ashamed of the gospel of Christ: for it is the power.
- Romans 14:17- For the kingdom of God is not meat and drink; but righteousness.
- Romans 15:19- Through mighty signs and wonders, by the power of the Spirit of God.
- 2 Corinthians 10:4,5- For the weapons of our warfare are not carnal, but mighty through.
- Mark 1:15- Repent you, and believe the gospel
- Galatians 1:6- I marvel that you are turning away so soon from Him who called you in the grace of Christ, to a different gospel, which is not another; but there are some who trouble you and want to pervert the gospel of Christ.
- 2 Corinthians- 11:4 For if he who comes preaches another Jesus whom we have not preached, or if you receive a different spirit

which you have not received, or a different gospel which you have not accepted—you may well put up with it.

- Revelation 19:15- Now out of His mouth goes a sharp sword, that with it He should strike the nations. And He Himself will rule them with a rod of iron. He Himself treads the winepress of the fierceness and wrath of Almighty God. And He has on His robe and on His thigh a name written.

Kingdom Saints-

The saint's agenda is to preach the kingdom, convert others to Kingdom by revealing the gospel(decree) of kingdom and manifesting its power on earth.

Daniel 2:34 says this mountain of Zion is a people. Mt Zion is a place of salvation, worship, learning and glory. Eph. 2:19 says we have become fellow citizens with the saints of the household of God. We are the place of God's rule, this rulership is in people, nations, and governments. Saints are called out ones who possess the kingdom. Daniel 7:18 depicts that the saints of the Most High shall receive the kingdom forever, even forever and forever. It is only received by Christ through FAITH

- Ephesians 2:10- For we are His workmanship, created in Christ Jesus for good works, which God prepared beforehand that we should walk in them.

CHAPTER TWO
KINGDOM ACQUISITION

Possessing our possessions is usually quoted to make a preaching point about material wealth and worldly accomplishments. I want to explore another prize that many have ignored or replaced with religious antics. David said in Psalm 16 that Jesus Himself was the portion of his inheritance and because of that David's lot was maintained by God. If we are going to acquire the kingdom then, we must not only define it but cherish it above other pursuits.

The acquisition of the kingdom is not just a formality it can be possessed in our spiritual heart, spiritual mind and as a natural inheritance. Yes, the kingdom can be possessed but not with the King of Kings revealing and permitting us to enter His domain. So, in embracing our spiritual rights of possessing the Kingdom let's clearly define the dominion of heaven and man.

Heaven's Dominion-

Heaven's Rule -We know that God is in complete control of and rules over the third heaven, and He also can rule over the first and second as He wills, but He allows others (us and Satan) to have dominion over the first and second heavens.

- Genesis 1:26- Then God said, "Let Us make man in Our image, according to Our likeness; let them have dominion over the fish of the sea, over the birds of the air, and over the cattle, over all the earth and over every creeping thing that creeps on the earth...
- Genesis 1:28- Then God blessed them, and God said to them, "Be fruitful and multiply; fill the earth and subdue it; have dominion over the fish of the sea, over the birds of the air, and over every living thing that moves on the earth.

The first Adam gave his dominion away to Satan, but the Second Adam gives it back to His people.

The heavens were created invisible environments (atmospheres) where one must live in spirit to experience them. There are invisible creatures that also live in the heavens – God's angels and Satan's fallen angels.

Man's Dominion-

Man's authority (dominion) is to function in three realms.

1. Earth – authority over the body (healing and prosperity) in the first heaven where one has world consciousness.

2. In the second heaven, one has self-consciousness. Soul / I will– As a result of thoughts and emotions either influenced by Satan or one's spirit man who is seated in heavenly place.

3. The third heaven is where we have God consciousness.

Man has been given the right to rule (self-control) in the first and second heaven. The Heavens were created as invisible environments (atmospheres) where one must live in spirit to experience them. There are invisible creatures that also live in the heavens – God's angels and Satan's fallen angels. The whole point of the heavens is to establish a right of rule (dominion). Will you establish yours and learn to experience these realms?

Kingdom Authority-

Apostolic people must know and understand the authority that is given by Christ.

- Matthew 10:1-42 - Jesus summoned His twelve disciples and gave them authority over unclean spirits, to cast them out, and to heal every kind of disease and every kind of sickness. Now the names of the twelve apostles are these: The first, Simon, who is called Peter, and Andrew his brother; and James the son of Zebedee, and John his brother; Philip and Bartholomew; Thomas and Matthew the tax collector; James the son of Alphaeus, and Thaddaeus; Simon the

Zealot, and Judas Iscariot, the one who betrayed Him.

Jesus operated from God's delegated authority to establish the kingdom of God during His time on earth. So, we too, as an Apostle will operate from this delegated authority. You can drive out spirits, subdue and set order in houses of God, ministries, and the earth due to this authority. This is the How.

Many times, the first thing one must set up in an organization is who can do what and what is the sphere of their authority. Likewise, as Jesus, was establishing His Kingdom on earth for Him to do the same. The question remains is have we been given license to act upon that authority delegated by Jesus.

I believe so, with Jesus leaving some, to do the work of building his kingdom aka church. The exercising of this authority relates and is expressed in power to make decisions, operate, and mandate certain things on the earth on His behalf. The mere concept of having an organizational hierarchy is for the smooth transition of chaos to peace, disorder to function and distributions of tasks to be accomplished.

Most times the head of an organization will leave someone in charge of overseeing and functioning while they are accomplishing another task that may be more important. So, case in point, we are here on the earth establishing Jesus's kingdom. What more important thing could Jesus be doing meanwhile? First, the bible says that Jesus is. seated at the right hand of the Father,

The bible says that he summoned them and gave them, to be summoned is to be called for a specific duty. Nowhere else is any other office of the fivefold summoned to authority but except in the Apostles.

- Luke 10:19 - Behold, I give unto you power to tread on serpents and scorpions, and over all the power of the enemy: and nothing shall by any means hurt you.

- Matthew 28:18- And Jesus came and spoke unto them, saying, All power is given unto me in heaven and in earth

Kingdom Power-

(Dunamis power, might and strength)

The Dunamis can do what man cannot do, and the legal claim to do it efficiently, immediately, spontaneously, and provokingly. It commands all of earth to yield to itself. Dunamis is what every believer has been given. How else can we overcome and bring Jesus' kingdom to earth, subdue the enemy, and take captives for Christ, unless we've been given POWER *

When you bring your need to the Lord in prayer, take the "if" out of your asking and pray in faith, expecting to receive! As Scripture promises, "The prayer of faith shall save the sick, and the Lord shall raise him up" James 5:15. It is God's will for you to walk in divine health and be in a right relationship with Him:

"Beloved, I wish above all things that thou mayest prosper and be in health, even as thy soul prospereth" 3 John 2. God assures us that He has not and will not change: "I am the Lord, I change not". Malachi 3:6.

Prayer Points for Ministers to begin moving in God's authority

- James 5:15- And the prayer of faith shall save the sick, and the Lord shall raise him up; and if he has committed sins, they shall be forgiven him.

- Mark 11:2 - Therefore I say unto you, What things soever ye desire, when ye pray, believe that ye receive [them], and ye shall have [them].

- Acts 3:1 - And his name through faith in his name hath made this man strong, whom ye see and know yea, the faith which is by him hath given him this perfect soundness in the presence of you all.

- Hebrews 11:6- And without faith it is impossible to please God, because anyone who comes to him must believe that he exists and that he rewards those who earnestly seek him.

- Ephesians 1:18-19 - I pray that the eyes of your heart may be enlightened in order that you may know the hope to which he has called you, the riches of his glorious inheritance in his holy people, 19 and his incomparably great power for us who believe. That power is the same as the mighty strength

CHAPTER THREE
FOUNDATIONS OF KINGDOM

For the kingdom of God is not in word, but in power (1 Corinthians 4:20).

The Mystery-

- Mark 4: 10- As soon as Jesus was alone with the Twelve and those around Him, they asked Him about the parable. *11* And He told them, "The mystery of the kingdom of God has been given to you, but to those on the outside, everything is expressed in parables, so that, 'they may be ever seeing but never perceiving, and ever hearing but never understanding; otherwise, they might turn and be forgiven.'

Apostolic Ministries, centers, people and culture must convert believers to the Kingdom. Please note there are requirements for true kingdom living.

- John 3:3 – Verily, verily I say unto you, except a man be born again he cannot see the Kingdom of God.
- Matthew 18:3 – Except ye become as little children, ye shall in no wise enter the Kingdom of Heaven.
- Luke 4:43 – And he [Jesus] said unto them, I must preach the kingdom of God to other cities also: for therefore am I sent.
- Luke 8:10 – And he [Jesus] said, Unto you it is given to know the mysteries of the kingdom of God.

God's Ekklesia is a Kingdom priesthood of all believers. Peter also captured this theme so well. He taught, using Old Testament language, that we, "as living stones, are being built up a spiritual house, a holy priesthood, to offer up spiritual sacrifices acceptable to God through Jesus Christ" (1 Peter 2:5). He then, marvelously, declared: "But you are a chosen generation, a royal priesthood, a holy nation, His own special people, that you may proclaim the praises of Him who called you out of darkness into His marvelous light" (1 Peter 2:9). The language is unmistakable. God's desire expressed in Exodus 19:5-6 is fulfilled in us!

The purpose of a priest is to minister to God and, of course, any true ministry to God overflows in ministry to others. The Old Testament priesthood was certainly involved in all kinds of ministry to people, but the point is obvious: the priesthood exists first and foremost to minister to God, not to serve as mediators between God and others. While God tolerated the second-hand, mediated relationship in the Old Covenant, He does not in the New Covenant. The New Covenant is a covenant sealed by the blood of His Son, the one and only Mediator, "For there is one God and one Mediator between God and men, the Man Christ Jesus" (1 Timothy 2:5).

Main Point- If you are going to operate in the kingdom of God's authority, convert others to this kingdom and take captives from the demonic kingdom, you must use the keys of the Kingdom. One overlooked key is the GOSPEL of the Kingdom.

- Mark 1:15- Repent you, and believe the gospel
- Galatians 1:6- I marvel that you are turning away so soon from Him who called you in the grace of Christ, to a different gospel, which is not another; but there are some who trouble you and want to pervert the gospel of Christ.

Another gospel- not of the Kingdom which is equal to the language of decree. Verse 8 says, *but even if we, or an angel from heaven, preach any other gospel to you than what we have preached to you, let him be accursed.*

We see many denominations lacking the Power of the Kingdom of the early saints/apostles. Could this be due to the tradition of man and denomination non-gospel of the kingdom teachings? JESUS TAUGHT THE GOSPEL OF THE KINGDOM. There is a ***BIG*** difference between the biblical gospel, man's gospel, denomination gospel and even the false gospel message.

- 2 Corinthians 11:4- For if he who comes preaches another Jesus whom we have not preached, or if you receive a different spirit which you have not received, or a different gospel which you have not accepted—you may well put up with it.

It is a part of every kingdom citizen to protect the laws, uphold the laws and wills of that kingdom's legislations and rulings. It is also the duty of every citizen to teach those who are ignorant of the kingdom's ways, along with exposing any treason against that kingdom.

Key Points of Understanding-

- We Must Preach the Kingdom via the Gospel of Jesus.
- We must convert those who are seeking the influence of apostolic ministry into the kingdom. This is not an overnight process, so patience is a key virtue in every apostolic team, father, mission, leader, and community.
- The kingdom of God is not just a reformation of the church, it is the way of God.
- The Kingdom of God shall invade the earth and we must submit to King Jesus as Lord over our ministries, concepts, denominations, and life.
- Everyone must be converted to the Kingdom of God, not to the church per se.
- Apostles pave the way, and pioneer nations, territories, and people to the kingdom of God using Jesus Gospel of the Kingdom and Jesus's delegated authority.

- Jesus is the head of His Ekklesia (cabinet) that He selects to govern the Kingdom of God upon the earth.
- Our primary mandate is to allow heaven to invade earth, reclaim all the citizens from Satan into the kingdom of God.
- We are comissioned to complete the work that Christ started on the earth and have been empowered by God via Jesus to operate in AUTHORITY to fulfill this assignment.
- There is just one HEAD of the Ekklesia Church appointed by God and the officers (five-fold leaders) can never be self or man appointed.
- These governing body members have authority to release power and govern the body, influence the nations, execute judgement, and restore peoples.
- You have been drafted into the kingdom of God once we accepted Jesus as Lord.

- All believers must become disciples who follow Jesus.
- Disciples are called into an office to lead other disciples and execute the will of God upon the earth. We are gifted to function within these offices.
- To operate in authority of Jesus we must remain submitted to Jesus.
- Authority has spheres of influence, i.e., statutes of limitations whereby it functions territorially, regionally, and corporately, but never independent of the will of God. God backs up His will by releasing the power to execute.
- Our wills must align with the Kingdom's will for our lives and ministry.

Apostles Function-

1. Taking the gospel to unreached areas. Paul said to the Romans, "It has always been my ambition to preach the gospel where Christ was not

known, so that I would not be building on someone else's foundation" (Romans 15:20).

2. Laying a firm foundation (Christ Himself) for the churches being established. Paul speaks of this important apostolic role, "By the grace God has given me, I laid a foundation as a wise master builder, and someone else is building on it. But each one should be careful how he builds. For no one can lay any foundation other than the one already laid, which is Jesus Christ" (1 Corinthians 3:10,11).

3. Training the initial leaders and appointing elders. When Paul and Barnabas made their second visit to Lystra, Iconium and Pisidian Antioch, they prayed and fasted and ordained elders in each church (Acts 14:21-23). Paul likewise instructs Titus to "set in order" the churches in Crete and appoint elders in every city (Titus 1:5).

4. Dealing with specific problems, false doctrines or sins in the churches that had been established. Paul's first letter to the Corinthians illustrates his use of apostolic authority to speak to a number of problems in the church he had planted at Corinth: disunity, immaturity, pride, immorality, taking other believers to court before secular authorities, questions about celibacy and marriage, disputes about meat sacrificed to idols, wrong handling of the Lord's Supper, misuse of spiritual gifts, confusion about the resurrection, etc.
5. Promoting unity in the Body of Christ. The unity principle was applied on many different levels. In Philippi, Paul had to deal with a situation of contention between two ladies in the local assembly, Euodia and Syntyche.[i] In Corinth, there was city-wide disunity in the church because of various believers choosing to rally around dynamic leaders such as Paul, Apollos,

and Peter. Paul also performed the apostolic role of providing a link of communication and sharing with the universal Body of Christ around the world.

6. Demonstrating and imparting the supernatural dimension of the Kingdom of God. Although it is God's intention for all believers to heal the sick, cast out demons and perform miracles by the power of the Holy Spirit, those in apostolic ministry particularly bear this credential. Thus, it is said that God did extraordinary miracles through Paul. Apostles were often used in a special way to impart the power of God to other believers (Laying on of Hands- Impartation, Activation of spiritual gifts).

CHAPTER FOUR
ACTUALIZATION

This is what we have all been waiting for, up to this point we have just been preparing for the vision to come to pass, but there is a time when it must manifest. This realm of bringing things from the invisible world into our earthly sphere or first heaven reality.

This is when our cup overflows. When the vision is a reality in our lives. If we have not gone through the first three steps we may delay the process, or even not bring the vision to pass. I want to submit to you that this is NOT God's job but ours. If this is the case that it is up to us to bring the vision to pass, this makes us Christians responsible and NOT God.

This should shift our paradigms of thinking because many have just thought that passively waiting would manifest their prophecy. Passively waiting for God to fix things, make it happen is a dangerous error. It is the same way we are saved by faith, however if we never walk out what we believe then we remain unchanged. Salvation is not a passive experience, neither is our self-actualization of our prophetic words from God.

- Habakkuk 2:2-4; And the LORD answered me, and said, Write the vision, and make it plain upon tables, that he may run that readeth it. For the vision is yet for an appointed time, but at the end it shall speak, and not lie: though it tarry, wait for it; because it will surely come, it will not tarry. Behold, his soul which is lifted up is not upright in him: but the just shall live by his faith.

Let us examine this scripture and see the details about this vision. First, the prophet was commanded to WRITE IT DOWN. The reason for writing was so that those that are around can read it and then grasp and run with it. Even if the prophecy is a personal vision about our destinies, we still should write it down, that was step two in this book.

Next is the concept of appointed time, this I believe is the set time of release based on God's timetable. I recently spoke with a Pastor that was believing God to sell their church and buy a new building. This pastor put the old church up for sale and not just, one year but three years went by before he found a buyer. At the same time, he happened to find a building that was available by divine connection the same month the old building sold. It all happened within two short weeks. I just strongly believe that we must learn to wait, patiently for God's APPOINTED TIME.

Until God's appointed time, no amount of persuasion from earth will bring it to pass before then. However, the prayers, intercession and faith steps will ensure it does come to pass. Remember, not everything that God wills is automatic, that's why Jesus taught us to pray God's will be done on the earth.

If you have completed all the steps diligently, then I believe you shall bring the prophecy to pass.

Do not forget to take faith steps and walk out by your ability what you can in faith.

Prayers To Bring it to Pass

John 3:16, 2 Corinthians 3:16

Heavenly Father, I thank You that you sent your only begotten son that I may have eternal life. Father I pray that You will remove the veil from my eyes that stops me from seeing Your true glory. Father, I ask that You reveal Yourself to me in a mighty way so that I will follow You all the days of my life and that I may dwell in Your presence, Amen.

Matthew 7:7, Exodus 33:18

Dear God, I thank You that your Word says to ask, and it will be given.[ii] Therefore, I ask today that You will show me Your glory God. May You also prepare me for all that You have in store for me that Your glory may dwell within me. God teach me how to walk in Your glory that You may dwell in me for the rest of my life, Amen.

Jeremiah 33:3

Dear Lord, I thank You for Your hidden secrets of prosperity that You have stored up for me. I pray that as I go to sleep tonight that I will dream dreams and have visions from You Lord. As I dream, I pray that You will manifest yourself to me and show me great and mighty things that I do not know. I pray that Your presence shall be evident in every area of my life, Amen.

James 4:8

Most Righteous Father to You I give thanks. Father I pray that You will help me to draw near to You, that You may draw near to me. As I draw nearer to You Father, I pray that You will manifest Your love in my life that I may know the true and living God that I serve.[iii] I also pray that You will manifest Your glory to those who do not know You that they may be saved, Amen.

1 John 1:5-7

To our Father, we give glory and thanks. Father I pray that You will help me to walk in Your light to have fellowship with You. Strengthen me in the areas that I am weak, that I may be always obedient to You. I pray that Your Holy Spirit will always dwell within me and that You will always reveal yourself to me that I may have an intimate relationship with

You Father, Amen.

Psalm 27:4, Acts 13:22

To our God and soon coming savior, I give You thanks. God, I pray today that You will reveal yourself to me and those in my life. May we have an encounter from the true and living God. I pray that the desires of our hearts shall be to seek after You that we may know You and that we will be men and women after God's own heart, Amen.

CHAPTER FIVE
LEADERSHIP EFFECTIVENESS

The efficacy of leadership in the apostolic model is a combination of tangible results, multiplication, demonstration of power and the distribution of resources. If we carefully examine them, we can see how to maximize our leadership capacity beyond our normal limits.

Leadership distribution-

"Your Apostolic Leadership is a distribution center"

- Acts 5:12- And by the hands of the apostles were many signs and wonders wrought among the people; (and they were all with one accord in Solomon's porch.)

Wealth distribution or resource distribution are all a part of a dynamic apostolic leadership skills. We must be good at allocating which resources are given to whom and the requirement of release. For instance, the leader himself is a resource, so he/she must be careful how they spend themselves. Careless expenditure of the grace, anointing and favor will not benefit the region or our realm of influence. A great example is when Jesus perceives His personal resource of anointing was being spent, he asked in response, who touched me? It was not a physical bother to Christ but a personal depletion of resources that had to be accounted for and qualified as beneficial to the kingdom. Just like our chief Apostle, Jesus, we will not spend ourselves without benefit to the global kingdom economy.

If our leadership is effective, we will distribute resources to the people within our influence and reach. The bible goes on to say that the cities surrounding the early apostle were impacted positively. The Bible says in Acts 5 -There came also a multitude out of the cities round about unto Jerusalem, bringing sick folks, and them which were vexed with unclean spirits: and they were healed everyone.

Every need was met, every-one was healed and the multitude out of the city was reached. Many people were healed, and the effect was the city rejoicing, however the religious leaders were not in favor of this kingdom liberation. The kingdom agenda prevailed.

Leadership Operations-

The kingdom operates just like any other military unit, with a strong chain of command and distinct personal and missions to accomplish its endeavors. Rules, regulations, and orders are not optional. OPERATIONS SHOULD NOT BE LED BY REVELATION.

- Galatians 2:2- And I went up by revelation and communicated unto them that gospel which I preach among the Gentiles, but privately to them which were of reputation, lest by any means I should run, or had run, in vain.

Paul is saying that he was led and moved by the revelation of God, and from that, he took the gospel to the gentiles. His apostolic operations were not mere associations of what he desired- his missions and operations were not man led. Apostles move by unction of God, not tradition, nor as men pleasers, neither according to their own wills.

Paul was commissioned by revelation directly from Jesus himself. He did not aspire to apostolic office, which we see many today doing. It was revealed to him.

- 1 Corinthians 15:7-9- "then He appeared to James, then to all the apostles; 8 and last of all, as to one untimely born, He appeared to me also. For I am the least of the apostles"

Apostolic Servant Leadership-

"A leader is not someone who is consumed with his own success and his own best interests. A true leader is someone who demonstrates to everyone around him that their interests are what most occupy his heart."

— John F. MacArthur Jr.

Apostles operate and minister with servant's heart, this is how the weightiness of the power is not intimidating to those who lead.

- Acts 19:21-22- After these things were ended, Paul purposed in the spirit, when he had passed through Macedonia and Achaia to go to Jerusalem, saying, After I have been there, I must also see Rome. So, he sent into Macedonia two of them that ministered to him, Timothy and Erastus; but he stayed in Asia for a season.

Paul completes the apostolic pattern of gathering, teaching, training, and sending. He chooses Timothy and Erastus, two of his spiritual sons that ministered to him, and sent them on an apostolic assignment. Erastus was not only a servant, but he was also a city manager (Romans 16:23). Until you have learned to serve someone else, you can never be a sent one. Minister, from the Greek *minus* or *minor*, means, "one who acts as an inferior agent in obedience or subservience to another; and one who serves or officiates in contrast to the master (magnus)." The most familiar English word describing a servant is the deacon. Someone once asked, "How do I know if I am a servant?" The answer is, "You find out when you are being treated like one."

Question:

What area of leadership are challenged in?

CHAPTER SIX
YOLKS OF YIELDING AND SUBMISSION

The foundational imprints of God's kingdom are found in the patterns that the early Apostles walked in. In this chapter we shall expound on the yolk of God and the burden of the kingdom. Apostolic leaders are yoked to Jesus' Kingdom versus tradition and religion.

Yoke - in the Hebrew are both used figuratively of severe bondage, or affliction, or subjection (Leviticus 26:13 ; 1 Kings 12:4 ; Isaiah 47:6 ; Lamentations 1:14 ; 3:27). In the New Testament the word "yoke" is also used to denote servitude (Matthew 11:29 Matthew 11:30 ; Acts 15:10 ; Galatians 5:1).iv

For our burden to be lighter, we must accept to be yoked together with Christ. Being yoked together with Christ means following in his footsteps and serving him faithfully. Jesus invites us to "learn from Him" which is the same as saying that we should be his disciple.[v]

To fully enter the kingdom our lives must be first follow the biblical patterns for success.

Apostolic doctrine is key to kingdom advancement. They continued steadfastly in the apostles' doctrine and fellowship, and in breaking of bread, and in prayers. Acts 2. If God is going to rule us through his kingdom inwardly, we must be following the apostolic doctrine given by our spiritual fathers. Every leader must distribute the kingdom principles with grace, care, and diligence.

The first order of God's kingdom is to convert us into disciples of Jesus Christ, which allows His spirit to reign in our hearts. This also allows for the kingdom of God to manifest itself in the lives of believers inwardly. So, the doctrine that we follow must be pure, the gospel of the kingdom, and not just religious antidotes. True disciples will continue not only in doctrine, but authority, teaching and instructions.

Those who are not submitted to the king have their own system of how to live. There are many philosophies of living that are accepted, and many of them are in rebellion to the rules of God. The first order of the kingdom is to set up rulership within our own hearts and souls, before we can make others into disciples, i.e., operate apostolically.

The reign of God is in the hearts of men: It does not come with pomp and splendor, like the reign of temporal kings which is merely to control the external "actions" and strike the senses of men with awe. God's reign is in the heart by the law of God; it sets up its dominion over the passions and brings every thought into captivity to the obedience of Christ. God's law is placed in our hearts through the new covenant.

- Jeremiah 31: 33- But this is the covenant that I will make with the house of Israel after those days, says the LORD: I will put My law in their minds, and write it on their hearts; and I will be their God, and they shall be My people.

God rules us through the establishment of His law in the heart.

- Romans 2:29- But he is a Jew who is one inwardly; and circumcision is that of the heart, in the Spirit, not in the letter; whose praise is not from men but from God.

The Pharisees were not submitted inwardly. They had the outward appearance of righteousness, but inwardly they were filled with wickedness. They were looking for an outward kingdom and missed the inward kingdom of Christ that transforms hearts.

- Luke 39: 52- Woe to you experts in the law, because you have taken away the key to knowledge. You yourselves have not entered, and you have hindered those who were entering.

Kingdom Revelation-

This inward rulership of the kingdom is the precursor for the knowledge of the kingdom. This is another of the spirits of Jesus from Isaiah 11, that we discussed previously. The spirit of wisdom and knowledge of Jesus is the necessary component to move in apostolic operations upon the earth.

There is a heavenly blueprint of pure kingdom ministry that comes exclusively from above, and the powers of darkness have fought for centuries to obscure or diminish the radicalism of this apostolic model of kingdom ministry.

Only now, in the early part of the 21st century, are we beginning to see the dawn of a new era of ministry that restores the 'heaven to earth' paradigm." John Mason

Apostles are master builders that carry the revelation of Christ's governing Church. As the apostolic ministry progresses, we will see a change from a pastoral-only model of ministry toward an effective apostolic model of ministry. Every transition has a process....

CHAPTER SEVEN

SYSTEMS AND STRATEGIES

Two important systems in the kingdom are sonship and multiplication. Ignorance of how these systems or principles work and one can completely abort his apostolic assignment and destiny. Sonship is the critical error that the enemy has been infiltrating through offense, selfishness, misunderstandings, and robbery.

Why? The answer is because we simply must inherit the spiritual DNA of Christ Jesus. So, there is a new sound, beat from which we move. We follow Christ and not the old natures. It starts with accepting Jesus as Lordship over our souls. This system means we can accept his ways, his love, his hope, his words and

discipline. It happens when we are no longer double minded. It means I have my being in Christ. Old things are passed away. Abide in me, and I in you. As the branch cannot bear fruit of itself, except it abide in the vine; no more can ye, except ye abide in me.

Our Father's invitation is to experience the fullness of His un-deserved grace and favor, (Ephesians 1:6) happens through sonship and adoption into the kingdom of God.

Sons and daughters generously extend grace to others' because they are not measuring themselves against carnal perceived standards. This is because they know the fullness of the Father's grace towards them. Sons and daughters respond well to measurements or reviews in work or ministry, knowing that they exist to call forth the best from the team.

The Father's Invitation

- John 1:12- Yet to all who did receive [Jesus], to those who believed

> in his name, he gave the right to become children of God.

Without the system of sonship and spiritual parenting the kingdom is not duplicated nor multiplied upon the earth. This is the only biblical means to pass down mantles, inheritances and reproduce men and women of God.

Any other form of ministry multiplication is just not apostolic in nature, nor does it stem from the branch of the Lord himself. For even Christ was the offspring of Jesse and the branch of king David, in the order of Melchizedek as a priest. Now once we have apostolic sons and daughters or have become aligned properly with a spiritual father there must be multiplication of the kingdom through these relationships. God says While the earth remaineth, seedtime and harvest, and cold and heat, and summer, and winter, and day and night shall not cease. (Genesis 8:22)

Once we understand dominion of heaven and earth, we have yet to allow God through submission of the outward layer of flesh to minister or express himself through us. Here are some key concepts every kingdom leader must embrace and teach his/her team. They are protocols or rules of engagement from Christ. If systems are the protocol, then strategies are our way to engage.

<u>Apostolic Protocols & Strategies-</u>

- Matthew 10:16-25- Behold, I send you out as sheep in the midst of wolves; so be shrewd as serpents and innocent as doves.

This speaks of persecution that we must be prepared to face. Many today, due to our modern culture, have become disillusioned, and have left the mission for lack of understanding and not taking heed to the WARNING of PERSECUTION. Jesus makes it clear that it shall come.

- Matthew 10:17-18- But beware of men, for they will hand you over to the courts and scourge you in their synagogues; 18 and you will even be brought before governors and kings for My sake, as a testimony to them and to the Gentiles.

Jesus also warns us to beware of MEN. Many today are wounded and sidetracked from the assignment because they TRUSTED in men versus GOD's instruction. We must never disobey God's instruction to follow the tradition of man.

- Matthew 10:19-20- But when they hand you over, do not worry about how or what you are to say; for it will be given you in that hour what you are to say. For it is not you who speak, but it is the Spirit of your Father who speaks in you.

WARNINGS Against Pride

- Matthew 10:24- A disciple is not above his teacher, nor a slave above his master.

We must speak what the Spirit has put in our mouths. We must drop our personal agendas for the will of God. Remember the story of Moses who did not fully obey and missed the promise.

- Matthew 10:21-25- Brother will betray brother to death, and a father his child; and children will rise up against parents and cause them to be put to death. "You will be hated by all because of My name, but it is the one who has endured to the end who will be saved. But whenever they persecute you in one city, flee to the next; for truly I say to you, you will not finish going through the cities of Israel until the Son of Man comes. It is enough for the disciple that he become like his teacher, and the slave like his master. If they have called the head of the house Beelzebub, how much more will they malign the members of his household.

Jesus did not warn us in order to incite fear in us, but for us to have foreknowledge and to strengthen our hearts in advance. This is what team training accomplishes for every apostolic believer.

We must prepare ourselves with fasting, watching, prayer and discipline.

CHAPTER EIGHT
APOSTOLIC TEAMS AND GENERATIONS

Apostolic teams are not necessarily made up of just apostles and prophets. They are a group of people that carry the "family mission" without selfish agendas. They are sent by their leadership and entrusted with delegated authority to establish God's rule in their realm of experience and expertise.

This is true of every Believer before God. But it is especially true of apostolic teams. "Setting aside personal agendas is a big part of the success of team ministry." ("NAR Apostle Bill Johnson explaining Apostolic Teams and ...") Many teams have failed in their mission because of an individual who wanted his/her gift or opinion to be recognized.[vi]

The Need for Others-

The revelation carried by Apostles and the five-fold ministry will

- 1 Corinthians 12:21-27- The eye cannot say to the hand, I don't need you!" And the head cannot say to the feet, I don't need you!" On the contrary, those parts of the body that seem to be weaker are indispensable, **and** the parts that we think are less honorable we treat with special honor. And the parts that are unpresentable are treated with special modesty, while our presentable parts need no special treatment. But God has put the body together, giving greater honor to the parts that lacked it, so that there should be no division in the body, but that its parts should have equal concern for each other. If one part suffers, every part suffers with it; if one part is honored, every part rejoices with it. Now you are the body of Christ, and each one of you is a part of it.

Let us examine what the scripture is saying here. The eye cannot say to the hand I don't need you! In other words, the Prophet (eye) cannot say to the hand (Pastor) I don't need you. (1 Corinthians 12:21)

Teams are necessary and is God's sovereign will for ministry. To operate otherwise is rebellion. The scripture goes on to say, *God has put the body together, giving honor to parts that lack honor.* So, we too must honor those parts of the body that lack honor. For example, we love to honor the Pastor and Prophet, but what about the Teacher? The teacher is a great gift to the body of Christ. However, many who are called to be teachers must be encouraged to stick to teaching and not try to become prophets. Our modern culture does not honor teaching, learning about the kingdom, so we must esteem them with honor. As apostles, we must encourage and honor the teachers, and activate them to their place within the body of Christ. This is God's apostolic order, His Kingdom mandate for apostolic teams within the body of Christ.

True Apostleship Always Involves Teams-

As we build people, we cannot forget that each must fit within a team. So, allowing ministers to remain rebellious and relationally dysfunctional is to go against God's order. Ministers in training who cannot operate as a team cannot be trusted with leadership.

- John 13:34- We must have love for one another, that is how the world knows that we are His disciples.

The scripture ends by saying if one part suffers, we all suffer and if one part rejoices, then we all rejoice. Apostolic teams must walk in unity, and this comes about when people are committed to walk in harmony with all brothers.

Allow God To Bring The Teammates-

In other words, God must assign your team to you, and this allows for them to have the prerequisite for the work, and the heart to carry it out. When we bind folks to our understanding, we limit the potential of what the team can accomplish

In order to properly understand and develop apostolic missions, churches and people, we must understand the functions of five-fold offices. This is how we can properly discern believers and appreciate their abilities within our gatherings.

- Ephesians 4:11-13- And he gave some, apostles; and some, prophets; and some, evangelists; and some, pastors, and teachers; For the perfecting of the saints, for the work of the ministry, for the edifying of the body of Christ: Till we all come in the unity of the faith, and of the knowledge of the Son of God, unto a perfect man, unto the measure of the stature of the fullness of Christ:

We see in Ephesians 4:11 five giftings or offices given by Christ. Verse eleven tells of the office, verse 12 tells of the reason these gifts are given and show how the trinity works with these gifts, and verse 13 parallels verse 12 in how these gifts function. We believe there are five gifting producing 4 functions. We also believe these gifting is evident today and all five are needed and in operation. Though some might be denied operation or tried to be not recognized, nonetheless, they do exist with limited exercised authority due to man's denial.

Training requires commitment and endurance on the parts of the trainer and trainee. Training requires us to go beyond just church service pew watching. We must allow our ministers or sons to come alongside of us and see our humanity. It requires they watch us while we do it, we minister together and then we watch and give feedback. If you are going to confer authority, then the ministers must have been proven first.

This is challenging work raising spiritual sons, but the reward is your legacy being established and sustained.

It's difficult for leaders to mentor with an old wineskin of religion, or with a heart full of heart and bitterness. We can and will be betrayed and we will sometimes pour into illegitimate sons, but once we've established a method that works, we can multiply ourselves in others and bear much fruit.

To really avoid the pitfalls of most teams, whether ministry, business or personal (family). We shall look at Franck Lencioni's 5 dysfunctions of a team.

The five dysfunctions are stacked in a pyramid and are hierarchical, much like Maslow's Hierarchy of Needs. Without building a strong foundation on the bottom, there is no achieving the higher-level goals.

Dysfunction #1: Absence of Trust

PROBLEM: This occurs when team members are reluctant to be vulnerable with one another and are unwilling to admit their mistakes, weaknesses, or need for help. Without a certain comfort level among team members, a foundation of trust is not possible.

SOLUTION: As the manager, set the good example by asking for help from your team members, admitting your own weaknesses and limitations, and be the first to own up to a mistake. When you take the lead, others will follow. Slowly, these habits will become culture and the team will begin to build the first unshakable brick in the pyramid — trust.

Dysfunction #2:
Fear of Conflict

PROBLEM: Teams that lack trust are incapable of engaging in unfiltered, passionate debate about key issues, causing situations where team conflict can easily turn into veiled discussions and back-channel comments. In a work setting where team members do not openly air their opinions, there is a lot of posturing and precious time is wasted, resulting in inferior decisions.

SOLUTION: Establish that conflict is welcome and purposeful. Define what healthy conflict looks like by praising healthy examples or giving corrective feedback if conflict veers towards unhealthy. You can also "mine for conflict" by opening a meeting with a bad idea to see if everyone will agree to avoid conflict and use this as a litmus test to open up healthy discussion.[vii] Lastly, you can designate a devil's advocate in a meeting, or use pro and con lists for ideas to get people to open up to sharing a differing perspective.

Dysfunction #3:
Lack of Commitment

PROBLEM: Without conflict, it is difficult for team members to commit to decisions, creating an environment where ambiguity prevails. Lack of direction and commitment can make employees, particularly star employees, disgruntled.

SOLUTION: Clarity and closure are paramount to overcome this dysfunction and move to the next level. Setting clear deadlines, reviewing key decisions at the end of meetings as well as what should and should not be communicated to other staff and contingency planning can help teams overcome their fears by creating clear plans and facing potential pitfalls and the fear of failure head on so everyone can commit.

Dysfunction #4:
Avoidance of Team Accountability

PROBLEM: When teams don't commit to a clear plan of action, even the most focused and driven individuals hesitate to call their peers on actions and behaviors that may seem counterproductive to the overall good of the team. This allows for mediocrity, poor performers to slip by and the leader to become the sole source of discipline.

SOLUTION: If teams have come this far, they have trust and commitment, then they will know that a team member calling them out not only has the right to do so because expectations and deadlines were clear, but that it is not a personal attack. This allows team members to confront difficult issues to hold each other accountable. Clear standards, progress reviews and team rewards are also important to make sure this area stays healthy.

Dysfunction #5:
Inattention to Team Objectives

PROBLEM: Team members naturally tend to put their own needs (ego, career development, recognition, etc.) ahead of the collective goals of the team when individuals aren't held accountable. If a team has lost sight of the need for achievement, the business suffers.

SOLUTION: When teams have a solid base of trust, healthy conflict, commitment, and team accountability and are recognized within the company for performance via praise or rewards, it will be easier for team members to put their own needs aside for the sake of the team. With these solutions, teams should be able to retain top performers, handle failure with resilience and stay focused.

Understanding the fivefold functions of believers will also help establish better functioning teams. I have listed some basic concepts to show how apostolic teams can assist each other.

The 5 Ministry Gifts Each Have Distinct Operations:

1. Apostles – *unity of the faith*
2. Prophets – *knowledge of the Son of God*
3. Evangelists – *bring us unto a perfect man*
4. Pastors – *bring us unto the measure of the stature of the fullness of Christ*
5. Teachers – *bring us unto the measure of the stature of the fullness of Christ*

These gifts Are Given for 3 Purposes:

1. To perfect the saints

   Perfecting – complete furnishing; equipping

2. For the work of the ministry

   Ministry – service; ministering

3. To edify the Body of Christ

   Edifying – build up; promote growth

Apostles – one who is sent

Prophets – interpreter of oracles that are hidden

Evangelist – bringer of good tidings

Pastors – shepherd ; herds man

Teachers – one fitted to teach; master; doctor

Questionnaire

Are you a catalyst?

Which chapter are you committed to implementing?

What are your goals?

Teams' dysfunction?

Apostolic Strategy from the book you can implement?

Do you need training, mentoring, affirmation?

Covering, Connection, Coaching?

Notes

Notes

For bookings, bookings, and more updates
from
Dr. Frederick Acklin
please visit:

www.Dr.FrederickAcklin.com

www.ingramcontent.com/pod-product-compliance
Lightning Source LLC
Chambersburg PA
CBHW062146100526
44589CB00014B/1696